BULL CITY

SLAM TEAM
DURHAM NC

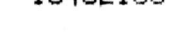

Write.Build.Succeed. Together
The Bull City Slam Team
ISBN (Trade pbk.)
978-1-7330502-3-4
Editing: Wendy Jones
Layout and Design: Dasan Ahanu
Cover Photo: Jackson Hall

HPJ's Writeeasy Publishing
Durham, North Carolina

www.bullcitypoetryslam.com

"A year, ten years from now, I'll remember this; not why, only that we were here like this, together." - poet, essayist, feminist, and National Book Award winner, Adrienne Rich

Table of Contents

write.build.succeed.
together
the bull city slam team

Brandon "iShine" Evans
"If A Mosquito Tells You He Can Pull A Plow, Don't Ask Him How; Just Hitch Him Up"

We still bless the ground with spirits
Because tears cannot be wasted

Even when the men cry here
It is the only time it is accepted
To shed tears
And not be called a pussy
Feels like a miracle

The casket's mouth is not
Wide enough to fit us all
So you told me, not yet boy
I know you smell cemetery
Breathe tombstone
Bed been grave
Been mouth hungry
And open
And waiting

The casket's mouth is not
Wide enough to fit us all
So we say you go first
All leathery and taut
Suit pressed like the day
You told my aunt
"Ain't no me, without you"

Aunt Lucille is 94
Burying her nephew
And I wonder how to live that long
And not tell the river
Here's my body, Do what you will
We cry not because you are gone
But because you did not take us with you

Too often
Black death is a surprise
A bullet's blind date with black flesh
A choke hold forgetting love lets go
We forget death does come
like a forgotten lover
A bed you once called home
But we still sing sorrow

Brandon "iShine" Evans
Percocets, Molly, Percocets

We be phoenixes
Learned how to turn a pill
into a lit match
And smile at the flames in our eyes
When the club is a field of dry grass
We will watch our bodies burn
And danced like the choking
was from smoke and not
Girls looking to find a home
in a bathroom stall

The girls still line up here
Like dominoes, pale bodies
dotted with black spots
up the arm
A game of numbers
A high for old men
With time to waste
And enough money
To turn a child into
a junkie

My uncle danced with the flame
My aunt still lights up
And smiles at the ash
we clean up after
Not the first time
her mouth gave a grin

3

when it meant to say help

And I'm here in this club
My friends look like moths
I am an apology
Forgiveness is my girlfriend
holding my shaking body
as I pray God lets me see morning

The sun rises
The fire took all the
oxygen out of me
And I'm still alive
I did not wake up
in a Hell that looked
like a dance floor
With all my friends
drowning in a sea
Of flames

Brandon "iShine" Evans
Ghost Stories

The way your face shriveled at the word mutt
tells me you ain't ever felt your existence spit
into the dirt
Never tried to make a portrait with everyone
else's definition of beautiful
Boy with unpronounceable skin
A failed attempt at Prometheus
Found out the people never needed light
Darkness was the default before you thought
yourself gods

Once a white girl told me I made her feel safe
And ever since then I understand how Chris
Brown still performs to sold out arenas
Like the sun will burn you but we got ointment
for that
Ain't no medicine for what men of night turn
white girls into
Make laws erupt from the bellys of frightened
fathers
Make prisons spring up from the ground like
forget-me-nots

Once I told my mirror I was beautiful
The glass cracked and blood seeped thru
Dripped onto the white tile
I call the day Apartheid

Rodney King dealt with alcoholism until his
death
And suicide is still seen as selfish
Like a man did not die on a street in LA
and arise a ghost
A banshee bent on reminding white folks that
they ain't free of us yet
I protested a black boy's death, knowing my face
would make politicians care about Black Lives
should an officer see the riot in my skin and
forget that whiteness is a chaser
I've been drunk since a white cop turned a skate
park into a history lesson
That is why my brothers don't let anything taint
the taste of Hennessy
That burn is Sojourner Truth reminding black
folks
it ain't what they call us
It is what the street sign will say about the
neighborhood built in your memory

She called me a mutt and a boy died on a street
in North Carolina
A wraith rose from his remains
Took his bones and built a haunted house
I know ghost stories are scary to those who ain't
seen death
That's why black people yell in movie theaters
and laugh at white folks not seeing the blade
coming like fate

Ashley Lumpkin
Sunflower

A man is dead,
and I am writing a poem again –
not a poem on the dead,
but on how I tire of writing these poems.
It is the fifth such poem I have written this year;
they don't have titles,
just hashtags and graves.
I tire of all the graves.

Down the street from my
apartment is an old cemetery.
They do not host burials there anymore –
the earth too filled with
bulky caskets to open itself up
to receive another.
The last time it did was a decade ago –
a little boy,
just six months old.

There was a ten-year-old in Jersey
chased by police for fitting the
description of some armed robber.
His neighbors surrounded him,
said, "This is a child," in the face
of those officers' loaded guns,
and no one died that day.
I was ready to write those poems.

I noticed there was no camera
there to capture the body's return
to the earth, and wondered if that

was the reason the boy was still alive?
What is the point of murder these
days, if no one can watch the killer
go free? How else to break a spirit
that knows they are coming for the
body? These bodies so much like the
earth. So full of bulky caskets – the
hashtags stacking up in the throat,
and no more room to receive them.

Every twenty-eight hours or so, the
little boy's father visits his grave – gives
him the name of heaven's next citizen,
and tells him bid them welcome. Tells
him how lucky he is to have left here
at six months old – with everyone
believing he is a child and not a criminal.
And not at gunpoint. With no poems
cluttered with hundreds of other names.
He has his own poem. His own grave.
I tire of all the graves.

I imagine how it would feel to write a
poem that didn't start in the cemetery.
Perhaps begins down the street inside
my apartment. There is a sunflower
I bought for my partner that sits on the
coffee table. It should have died weeks
ago, but it is still alive. How else to
remind the spirit that no one has say on
its right to be here. To grow, to flourish
in spite of. To still be alive.

Ashley Lumpkin
Genesis

When your God,
as you say,
created the earth,
He made it a perfect sphere.
Us calling it flat had no bearing
on the weight and round of it;
our seeing an edge did not make
the horizon any less an arc –
and you call you daughter
your son.
Don't you see?

She was made perfect His way.
Being born in a body
that you call boy has no bearing
on the truth and girl of her.
What privilege are you invoking
to preserve what has always been a lie?
Have you heard there are those among us
who still believe in a flat Earth?
Still require some proof beyond all that has been
seen?

When your God,
as you say,
created the earth,
He said, "Let there be,"
and so it was.
She has said to us all,
"This is who I am."
And so it is.
And it is good.

Ashley Lumpkin
Jezebel

When he asks if I spit or swallow, I tell him I am
a preacher's daughter.
He laughs because everyone knows daddy's'
girls with God issues give the best head.
We learn first how to get on our knees.
How to make miracles with our mouths.
How prayer is performance that testifies too
much to happy ending.
Say "Hallelujah" when you come, and they will
call you unholy,
But heaven ain't the only thing metaphored too
much as a pearl.
So sex happens.
And he enjoys it.
And I think about prostitution too much to talk
about with any levity because some things are
not a joke.
Like how I've taught three teenage girls I *know*
engage in sex work –
Their bodies the paychecks counted on to keep
the home heated.
And I am partly on this date because the fridge
here is empty.
And there are those in the world who think that
is the same thing.

He says, "I want to hold you until you fall
asleep."
I say, "I'll respect you more if you leave when I'm

awake;
You know the Bible says, 'Watch and pray.'"
Go in eyes open to the God who gives exactly
what you ask him for,
Even when receiving is hard;
Even when you tell him to go away;
Even when you know you brought thieves to the
temple; it hurts when he leaves with fists full of
spare change.
Did you know Jezebel was a preacher's kid too?

In her version of the story she wanted to burn
the incense for altar at temple.
She wanted to be the thing to cover the stench
of sacrifice;
So when the day finally came for her to die for
all God's people,
She did with her best dress on and make up on
her face.
Ain't that just like a good woman?
To brave the sight of what's coming?
To see death approaching and still put a smile
on anyway?
Get all dolled up anyway?
They will treat you like plaything anyway, so
you'd better know the rules.

When I ask him to leave, he hears a
blasphemer's tongue calling me unholy.
And what better way to absolve himself than by
calling me a whore?
A thing more tease than taste, more talk than

touch - a lamb worthy of sacrifice but unworthy
of forgiveness.
They will ask how short the wool; how rough the
shear; how loud the screaming -
Was there any screaming or did you just say
"Amen?"
The word "amen," is said to mean "it is so."

And it is.

The next morning, I am still a preacher's
daughter - still a Jezebel wrapped in Gabriel's
skin -
A halo tucked around the things they say will
send me to hell.
And perhaps, I learned to pray wrong,
But I am teaching myself to forgive.
Each poem scything the shame away from this
body,
offered as sacrament.

Ayanna Albertson
Depression

It's hard to express that you're depressed When
the only acceptance of depression is after you've
gone to the extreme

After IVs branch out your veins like trees and
your sanity takes an extended leave

But tell me,

Am I any less depressed if I don't want to die?
Does anxiety not apply if I've never
contemplated suicide?
If I enjoy my life...
but somehow hate it at the same time?

Truth is,
I've never slit my wrist
Never overdosed on pills
On most days, I feel absolutely okay
But on days when I'm not, I feel it heavily...

Ayanna Albertson
My Rapist

My rapist doesn't know he's a rapist.
In fact, he calls what happened that night sex
Says
We should hook up again some time
Can't seem to wrap his mind around why I won't
reply to his text

His eyes were bloodshot red
His breath reeked of booze
Pressed drunk dead weight against my small
frame
Chained my wrist together with one hand
Too intoxicated to comprehend my "stop" or
"no"

I've never seen a clock move so slow
He burglarized this home & still don't know he a
thief
Stole power over my own body
Assumed my invite over was consent
Consumed so much liquor don't even remember
what he did
Didn't even ask my how my day was going
Won't interested in knowing if I was interested in
him

Can you imagine?
Trying to find forgiveness for someone who don't
even know why they should be sorry?

Knowing he may read this poem and still not
realize he's the villain in this horror story?

Tell me,
How do you tell a monster he's a monster when
can't even recall the night he made you victim?
When the alcohol in his system made amnesia
of his assault
Who's at fault?
When he, too wasted to feel guilt
And me, guilty of being too much woman to
resist?

I wonder if he has kids now?
If he teaches them to respect other people's
property?
To keep their hands to themselves?

I wonder if I'll ever tell?
If I'll ever forgive myself for keeping silent?

All I know is...
If it's one thing that I've learned,
It's that the worse pain came from surviving.

Ayanna Albertson
I believe in love like I believe in God

I believe in love like I believe in God
That both, although intangible, can still be felt...
seen
It seems as though neither are as pursued as
they use to be
I still believe in chivalry
Having the courtesy to open doors & pull out
seats

That purity is the greatest gift you can give &
receive

I still believe in marriage
In two becoming one
In you becoming mine
in the butterflies that congregate on the inside
when his or her name finds its way to your ears
In the years of failed attempts that equip you for
your God sent
Like when God sent His son to die for our sins

I still believe in sacrifice...
In grace being sufficient
In asking a father for permission to make his
daughter your bride

I believe that love is divine...
So let me be your heaven on earth
Allow me to prove to you that marriages work

16

In a world
Where God and love have taken a backseat
I still believe in their ability to free a dying soul

Let's grow old together.

And even when stormy weather comes to rain
on our parade,
I pray you'll be a storm chaser
Still pursuing this love every step of the way

On the days,
When our home has turned into a war zone and
our words become weapons,
may we never question the reason we fought for
us in the first place

I still believe in first dates
With the same person ...
Over
and over again.

That your spouse should be your best friend
And the first person you confide in

I still in believe in compliments
Like
"Thank God for oxygen because you're breath
taking"

I still believe in praying
That if God be for us, then who can be against?

That a kiss is exchanged between eyes long
before the lips touch
I will always believe in us

'Cause I believe in love like I believe in God

That both, although omnipresent, have a way of
showing up just when you're in need

That both, although intangible can still be felt

Seen

It seems as though neither are as pursued as
they use to be

But I choose to be yours

& His

For the rest of my life

& the eternal one that follows.

Eric Thompson
To be

To be black
Is to be fertile ground
Producer of a world
That the farmer takes credit for
A farmer whose job it is to
Treat your earth with ownership
Point at your living and call it wild
Take your natural and force it into rows
Than calls it crop to say it has value now
Say your yield grows better with pesticides
Change your title but still not let you grow free
Ain't that healthier
Ain't it organic
But wait now they own your seed
Anything they do it belongs to him
And to his kids
That's how you got hand me downs
From germination to generation
That's how they grow inheritance
It's a dirty job but somebody has to do it
To be black is to be fertile soil
In a place where everyone wants to eat
But nobody wants you to sit at the table

Eric Thompson
Awkward Visitations

My key don't work no more
Front door was told
Not to unlock to strangers
Only accept whispering knuckles
Waves for those in inside

I still keep it though
I like to think
Broken still has purpose
I like to think
that somebody's home
That my face is key enough
That my family isn't outside
That the people living in rooms
Left this light on for me

They heard that my heart
Might have need a roof one day
So they kept our memories in the attic
Stored our shoes in the basement
Wrote down my address
the same way they spelled my name

I wonder if my mother
Still laughs
As beautiful as water falls
Is my father's wit
Still the gravity that clings to
Do they still palate song and worship

Does sunday morning still
Eat before everyone else

I never knew what is was to go hungry
And when i did there was food to eat
I never knew what it was to be lonely
And when did it was cause we did not speak
Even now I am starting to miss our silence
How the porch spoke like an introduction
How our smiles worked like lock and key

Eric Thompson
How Our Hugs Always Opened

Seven

For when God performs a c section on the sky to
pull my mother from this world to birth her into
heaven, seven moments to hold on to

One,
when I was blue sky
Barely over horizon
Learning to use windy words
To move cumulus cloudy no's
In front of sunshine commandments
My mother
she told me to read a poem
I told her
no
she responded summer breeze swift
bringing chills to my disobediences
I have learned that forever
when my creator gives me a poem
I will read

Two,
When the shadow of my
First failure followed
My mother showed me
that the sun will always set
but moon will rise
there will always be another day

Three,
 In car with silence turned up
Just above our distance
A radio comedian referenced his privates
I abbreviate our space with laughter
My mother asked
you don't think i know what he's talking about,
do you?
She laughs and says
His penis
A dick joke with mom
We share this umbilical cord of laughter
together dining on healing

Four,
9 pm
friday nights
watching X-files

Five,
When mom invited God home after revivals
he always woke the house
silent lessons in
feeling the unheard

Six,
I mistaken not being told about grandma
for sunday secrets
My mom taught me
that the recipe of heartache
can only be share

when you have prepared it yourself
first

Seven,
when arguments painted the walls
A brittle matrimony
love became a symbol of misdirection
My mother reminded me
we are the descendants of a carpenter
you can either hang on the cross
or build with it

Wendy Jones
Mangled

I imagine our first kiss
a combination of honeysuckles, razorblades and
train wrecks
full of nervous laughs
The universe will mock us
the stars play hide n seek with the clouds
We made the man in the moon smile
you will hold my hand
tracing the lifeline in my palm
trying to find where you fit
One day this will become complicated
there will be silence
our doubts will remain stuck in our throats
strangled by fear
There will be declarations of guilt
Questions for God
And a moment of clarity
That reminds us
Time is limited & far too precious to be wasted
on silly things
Like hesitation
Like believing in magic
Like reality
But for now...
We will have our first kiss
A fairytale moment that even Disney couldn't put
a visual on
A moment that even a car crash couldn't

metaphor beautiful
A second that will make heaven seem like hell
Our first kiss will be a memory of
New butterflies unquestioning their own wings
Enough to realize flying is better than sitting still
It will be guiltless
It will be trusting someone enough to suck your
heart right out of your chest
And know they will keep it lodged to the roof of
their mouth as long as they live
It will be having faith in you enough not to break
me
It will be forever

Wendy Jones
Truth or Dare

I know how this happened how we got here
I also know that it happened quite fast
so in case you don't, let me remind you......
It started....
Somewhere between sharing my inner most
secrets
And a game of truth or dare
Dare: was a kiss
Truth: is I want you....
I want you to love me like you love her
I know that I will never be her, but I envy her
I want you to write poems about how much you'll
miss me when I'm gone
I want you to be there in the middle of the night
when I've had a bad dream
and us, well....
I want us to spend lazy Sundays wrapped up in
only each other
I want us to talk about our future together...
I want us to have pet names for one another
in the morning I will call you my Sunshine and at
night my Starlight
I dream about "us"
but unbeknownst to me
this was a competition
and I was way out of my league
See I always lose at this game......always
You...
you never asked for my heart

(for you have a quite a collection already)
but me,
I gave it anyway
strategically placing it at your feet
whether by accident or on purpose
in perfect position to be trampled on by you
I should have just said "here, put it on the shelf
right next to that one....no, no, no over there,
yeah that's perfect."
but no, how dare I go up on the shelf with the
others
foolishly thinking this time I could win
You'll say you didn't mean to hurt me
didn't see my heart at your feet
and the trampling
well, that was all just a big misunderstanding
and some days......
some days I will believe that
it doesn't make it hurt any less
but for a brief moment I forget about the pain
and then I remember....

Truth: You,
you will never love me like you love her
and I'm okay with that because I will never be
her
you will never write poems about how much you
miss me when I'm gone or how much you love
me
you will never be there in the middle of the night
when I've had a bad dream and me,
well.....I choose

Dare: I have strategically placed my heart at
your feet
this time carefully wrapped with a note that says
"fragile, contents break easily" as if an offering
to the Goddess of Mercy
praying....that this time you will be more careful
that this time I will be strong enough to just be
your friend
Truth: I've never been afraid of roller coasters
the twists and turns never bothered me
the fall is all that scares me
the bumps and bruises are battle scars I know
too well
but for you I will try to hide them
you should never know just how easily I shatter
I wear them proudly as if to say "look at me, I'm
strong"
knowing that in reality I'm as fragile as the
butterflies still fluttering in my stomach every
time you walk in a room
your turn............Truth or Dare?

Wendy Jones

The Aftermath: How to Survive After Losing Your Best Friend

One.
Repeat.
Every morning remind yourself that he is gone.
Let's be honest, you always knew that Batman
was mortal.

Two.
Love.
He's the only person who has ever seen you this
broken.
Be patient with your friends, they will offer to
"stand in his place" - they don't know what else
to do.
They mean no harm, be careful with how you
turn them down - they're all you have left now.

Three.
Warn.
There's a quarry where your heart used to be.
Those who dare enter will be lost in its turmoil -
it's your responsibility to warn them of the
dangers.
Even the ones who break through the stones will
eventually drown in the pit.

Four.
Indulge.
Have casual sex.

Often.
Don't get attached.
The passion will remind you that you're still alive
- If only for that moment.
Pretend he's watching - it's what he would want
Worry about the emptiness later.

Five.
Watch.
YouTube is your friend.
He's alive there.
He still laughs there.
He loves there.
Save all of his videos, watch them regularly.
It'll help you forget he's gone.

Six.
Imbibe.
Vodka will replace late night phone calls.
Okay, not really, but it will definitely make sleep
easier to find.
On the quietest of the nights if you listen
carefully you can still hear him whisper
"goodnight Beloved Moon"
Pay attention -

Seven.
Entertain.
Play with new boys (and old) - Give them
nicknames like Goober, Unicorn, Sunshine...
Love.

They are all things you don't believe in; It'll make
it easier when they leave.
They always leave -

Eight.
Surrender.
The urge to cry will often come upon you - give
in.
There's a raging river behind your eyes.
The dam will break with no warning -
While driving - while cooking - while breathing
Soon it won't seem that odd, you'll learn to deal.

Nine.
Nine. Neuf. Nove. Nueve.
You had nine years together - be grateful.

Ten.
Pray.
It's been 133 days since you last spoke with
God -
She's not the enemy.
Remember "I God you" is more than just a pretty
metaphor.

Eleven.
Accept.
He is gone.
Say it aloud.
Tell everybody, whether they ask or not -

Twelve.
Forgive.
Him. God. Yourself…. forgive.

Thirteen
Fight.
You will want to die -
You will try to die -
You will survive -
He is a part of you-
Always.

Dasan Ahanu
Glass Cases

We be the children of glass blowers.
Pious crafters who work
with hands clasped together and
knees touching the earth.
Earth that taught them how
to bear fruit, birth things that grow,
and give to others
until they die.
Glass blowers whose wishes
to the carpenter
that sits on high
become part and parcel promises,
components of glass cases
covering us in grace.

We pieces of wonder...
We be knick knack,
trophy, and
admirable qualities well sewn together
and draped on mannequins.
We be fine china,
snapshots of happy and unsure, and
memories of times past
longing for tomorrow to come.
We be the things none have had
or that others have had but
no longer want.

We sit on thrones

that become tombs and
on stages that
become prisons.
The plate at the bottom
holds the names we are given
but may or may not have earned.
It sits there until replaced
by numbers, a dash, and
remembrances rewritten
by guilt and could have beens.

The spots you notice on the outside
are not bruises.
They are the smudges
I pray the next caretaker
will Windex clean.
What's in here is priceless
but closed off.
Too many have fiddled
with the lock hoping to
pry openness and
expose what's inside.
Some have even tried the smash
and grab hoping to bully
their way in.
Thank God our mothers have
unwavering faith.
They have prayed and cried
until the vision of us is
shatterproof, bulletproof,
though still not protected
from the trauma of seeing

the attempts come and go.
Why won't they learn that
they key is in our eyes?

When your purpose and destiny,
worth and wisdom,
aptitude and ability
are on display
you learn what a fetishizing gaze
feels like.
You learn that gawking
is a seductive
dance with voyeurs whose
admiration is a selfish satisfaction.
That sometimes presence
isn't possibility,
it's just momentary possession.
Without the key though,
it's just a traveling exhibition.

You and me,
we know these glass cases
oh too well.
These cursed gifts
of safe distance and deniability.
We know too many living rooms
we never considered home,
too many bedrooms
we never felt completely comfortable in.
We have felt trapped in hallways
where people seem too eager
to pass our pain by.

Know too well that shrines
can be adored or despised
but still left to dust or decay.

We be held on to
for others to enjoy.
We be look but don't touch.
We be window shopping fantasy.
That one day I'll be able
to get that.
That I don't know if that's for me.
We be looked at.
Look at that.
Come here and look at this.
Look now.
Look later.
Walk past with nose up
and never look at all.
Arrogant assurance telling yourself
that it'll be there
when I want to look again.

We
the children of glass blowers.
We be here.
Help up by divinity,
shielded by hope
in glass cases
for all the world
to see